GREATEST PIANO THEMES FROM THE MOVIES

Cherry Lane Music Company
Director of Publications/Project Supervisor: Mark Phillips

ISBN 978-1-60378-953-0

Visit our website at www.cherrylaneprint.com

American Beauty

from AMERICAN BEAUTY

Music by Thomas Newman

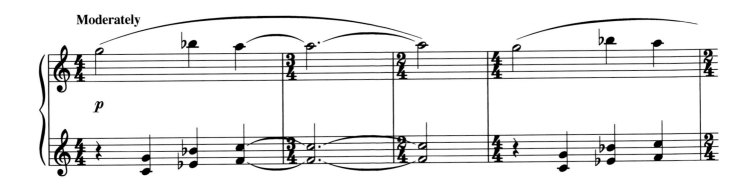

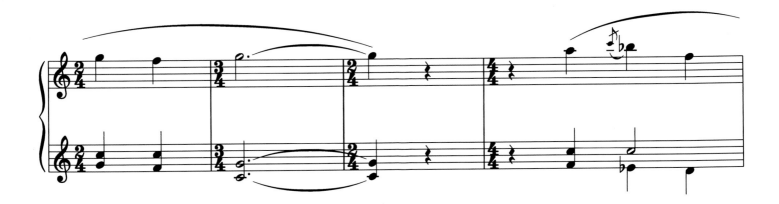

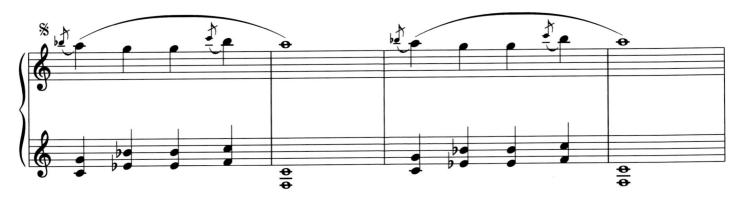

To Coda

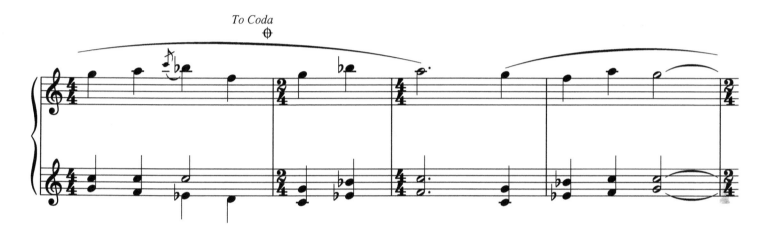

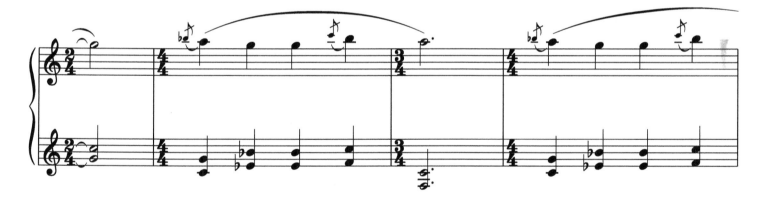

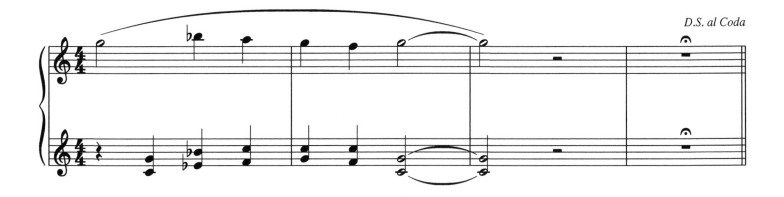

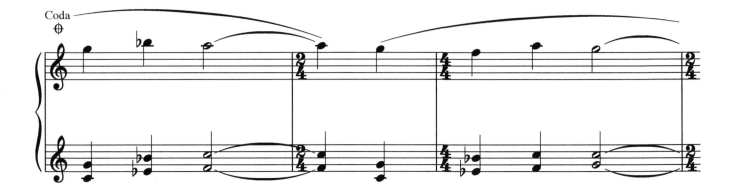

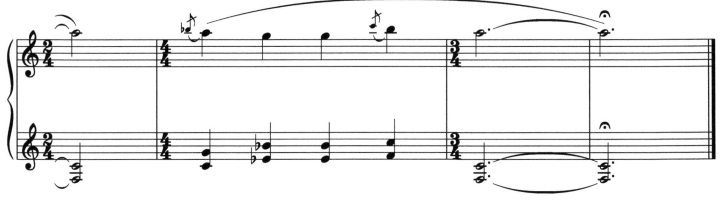

4

Chariots of Fire

from CHARIOTS OF FIRE

By Vangelis

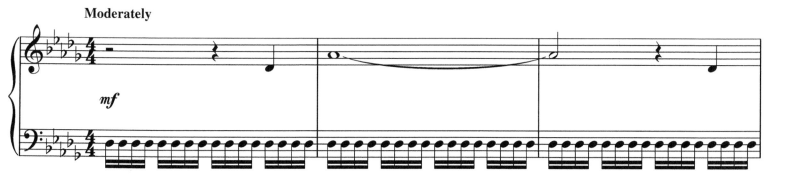

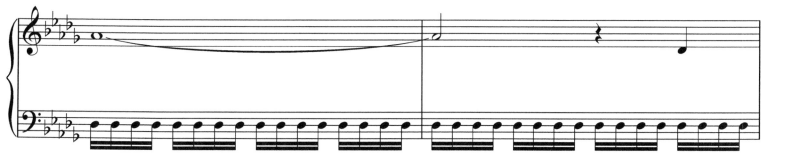

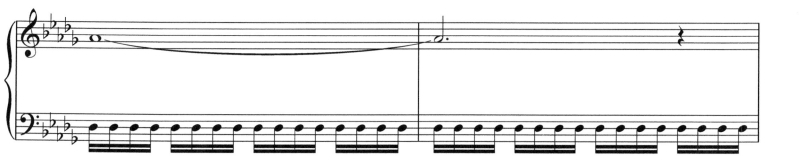

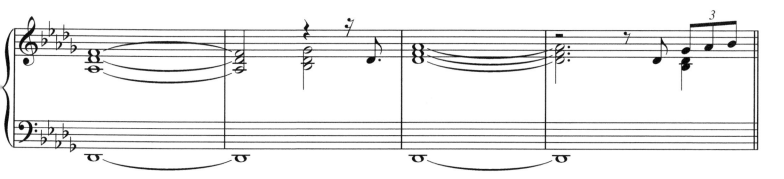

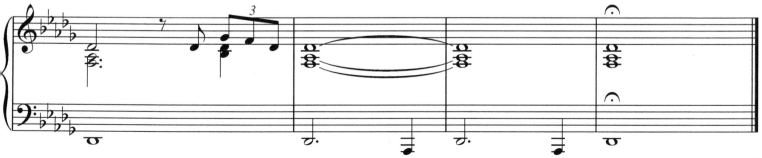

Chocolat
(Main Titles)
from the Motion Picture CHOCOLAT

By Rachel Portman

Slowly, expressively

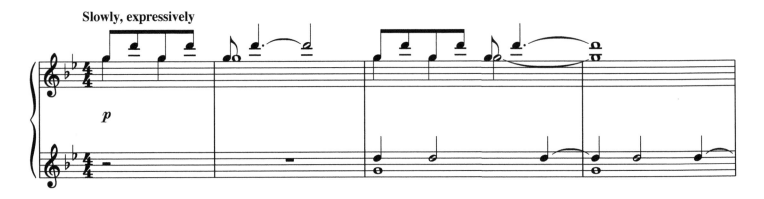

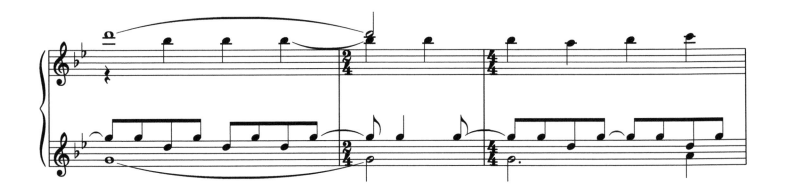

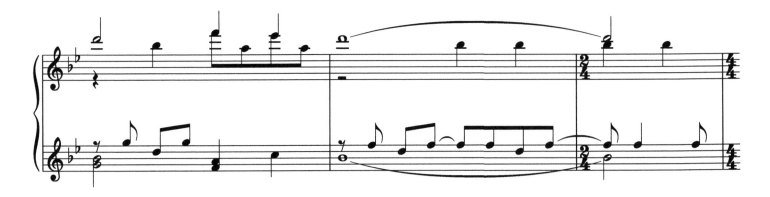

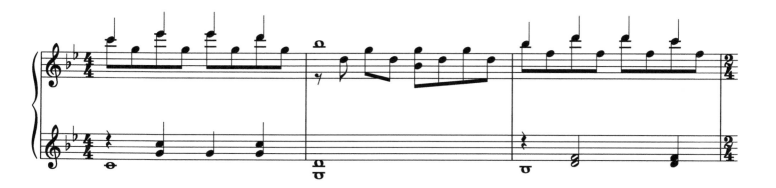

rit.   a tempo

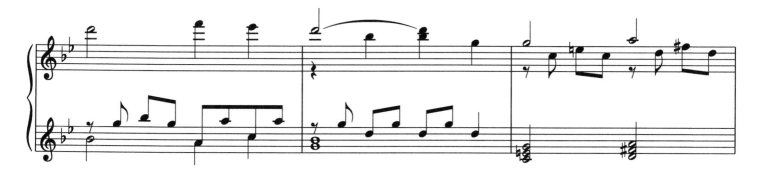

Moderately, in 2

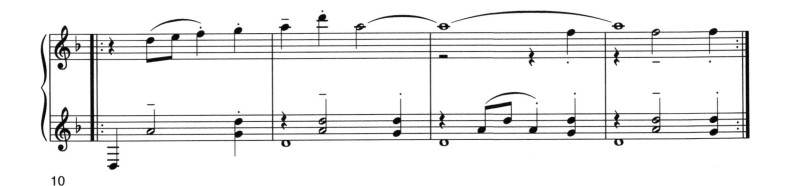

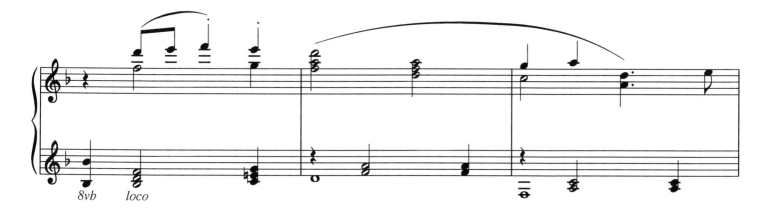

8vb   loco

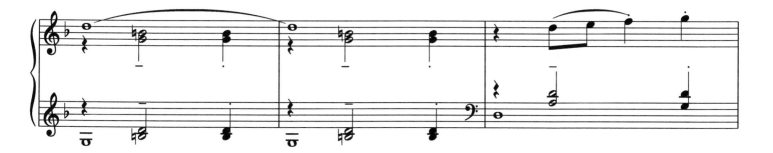

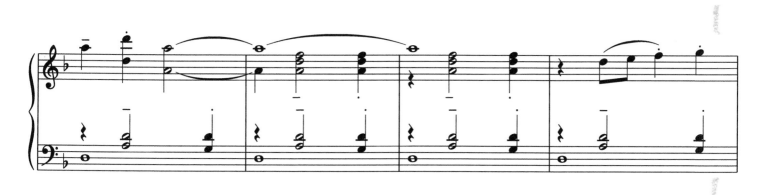

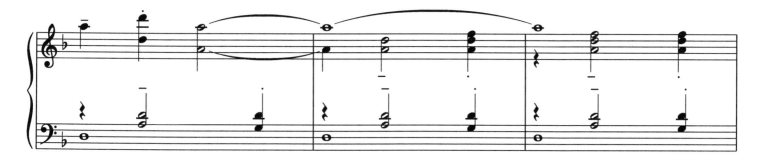

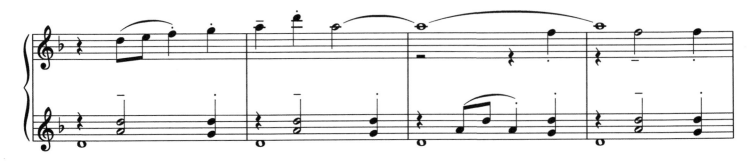

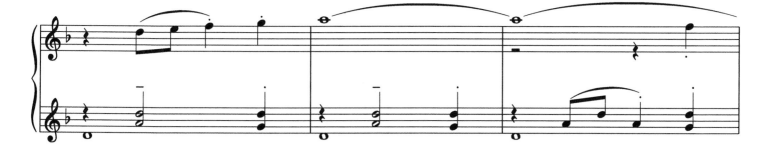

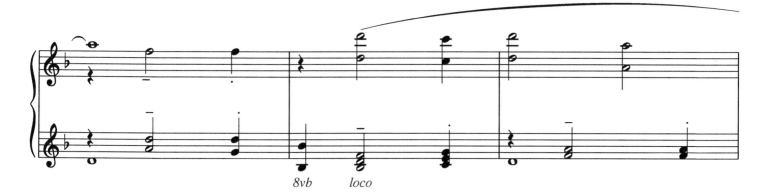

8vb   *loco*

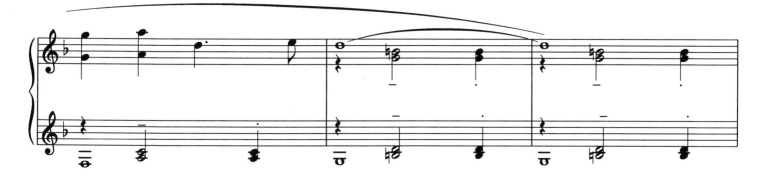

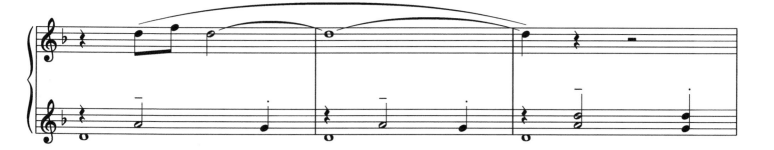

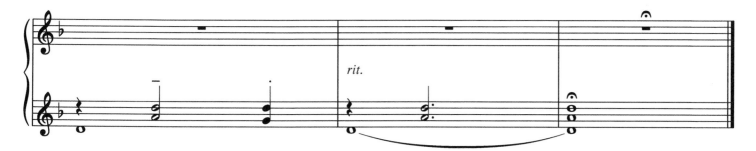

rit.

The Cider House Rules

(Main Titles)

from the Miramax Motion Picture THE CIDER HOUSE RULES

By Rachel Portman

Moderately

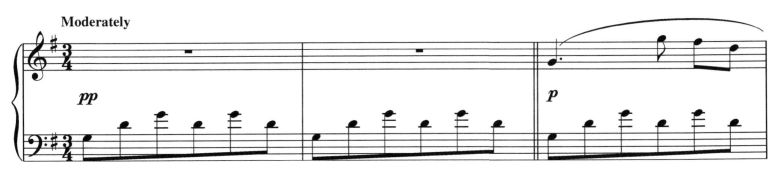

With pedal throughout

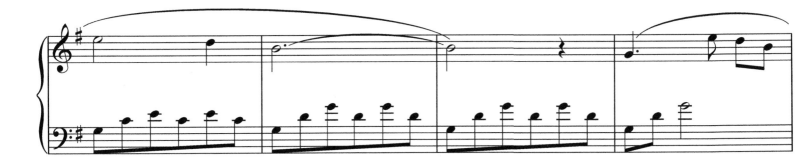

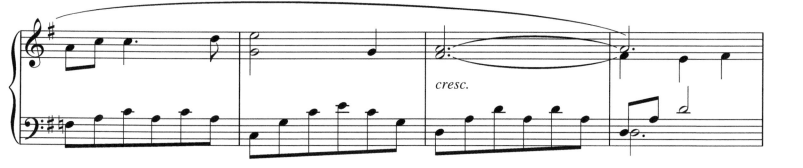

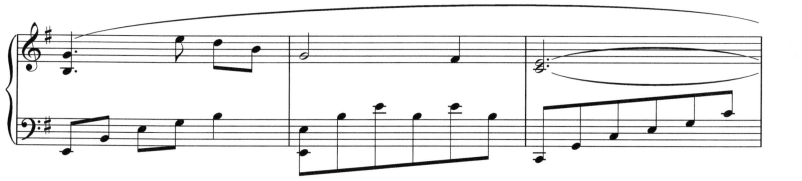

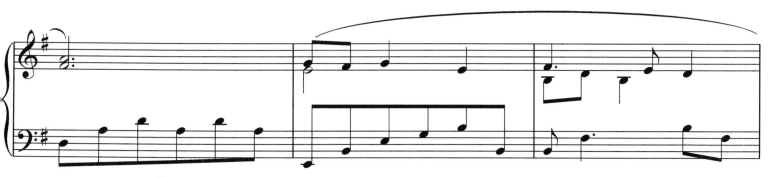

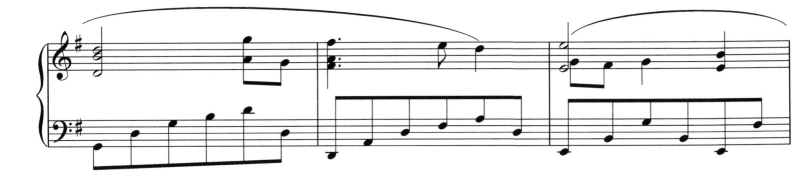

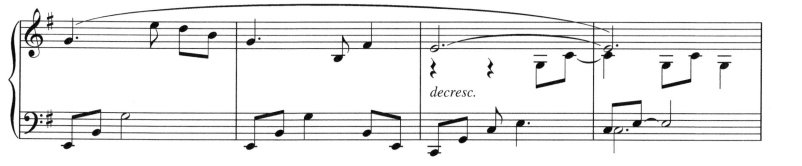

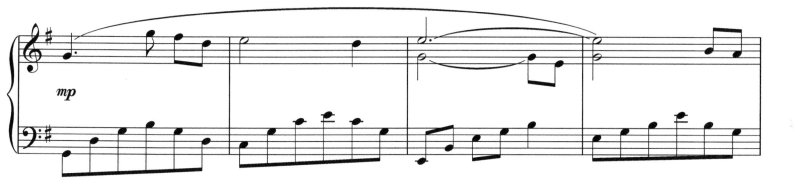

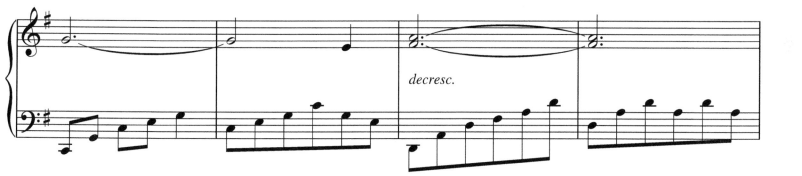

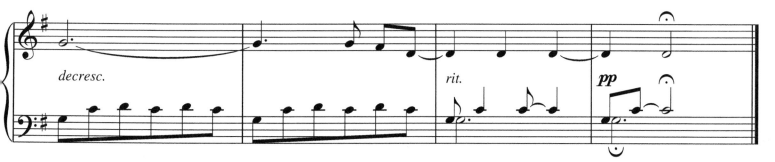

Dawn
from PRIDE & PREJUDICE

By Dario Marianelli

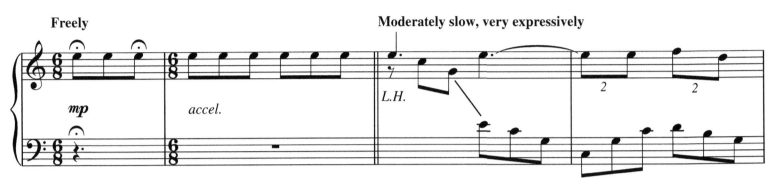

rit.

Slightly slower

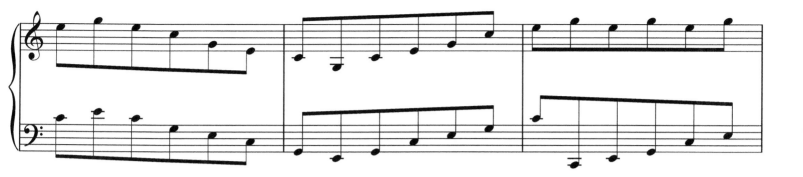

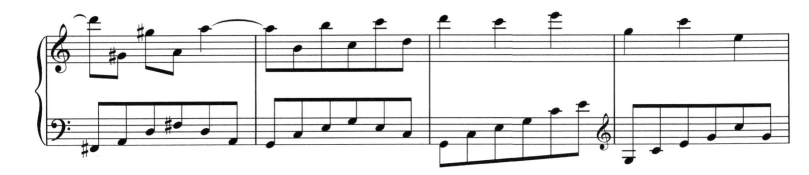

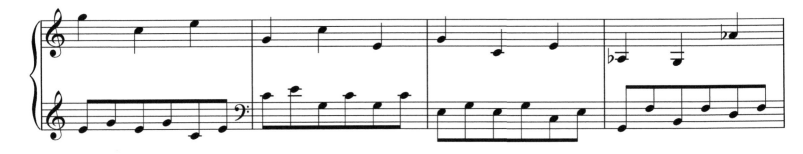

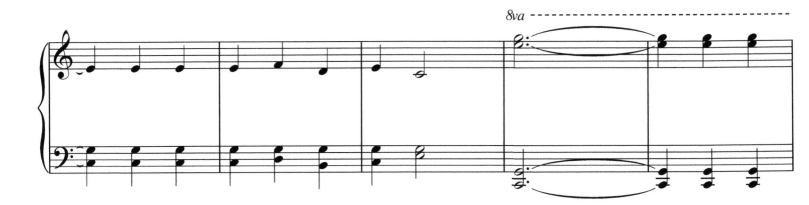

The Firm – Main Title

from the Paramount Motion Picture THE FIRM

By Dave Grusin

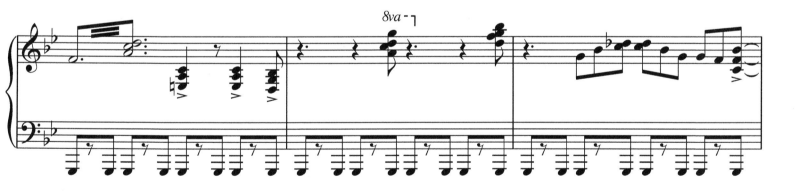

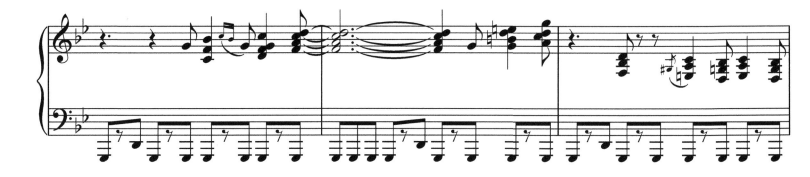

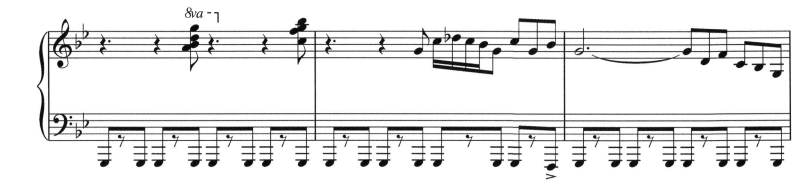

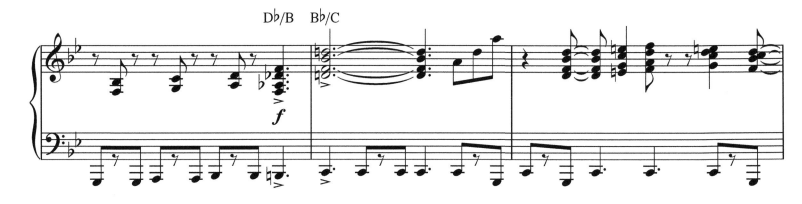

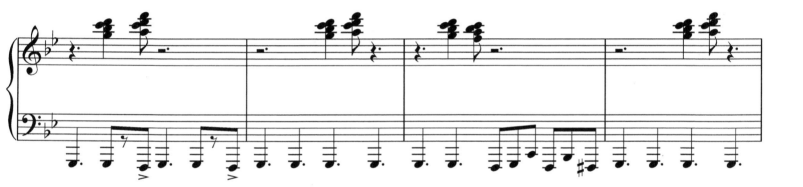

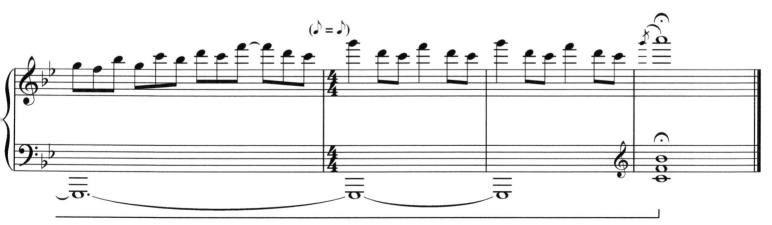

Georgiana
from PRIDE & PREJUDICE

By Dario Marianelli

Moderately fast, in 4

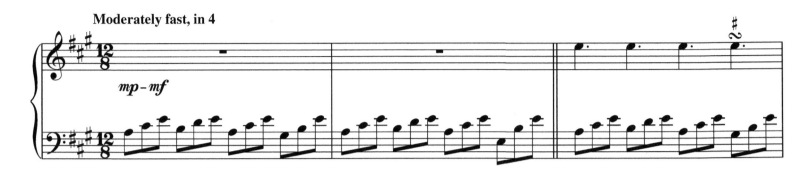

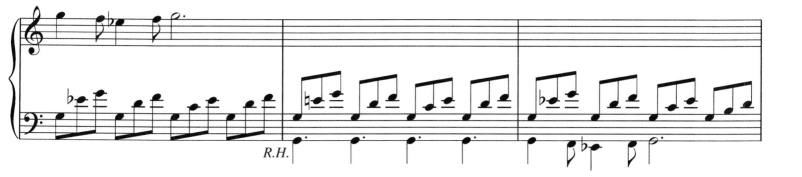

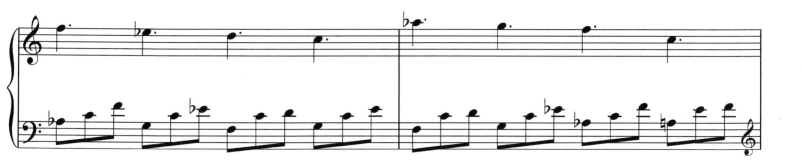

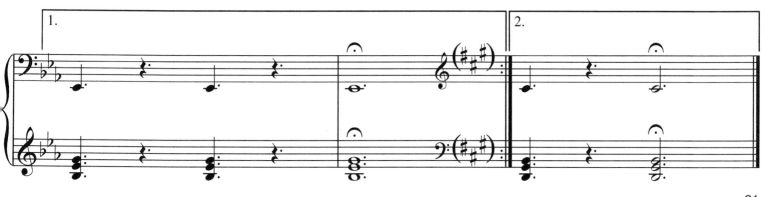

Forrest Gump – Main Title

(Feather Theme)

from the Paramount Motion Picture FORREST GUMP

Music by Alan Silvestri

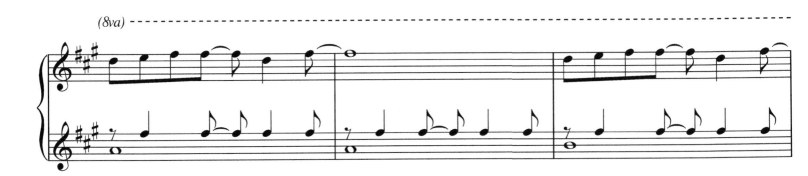

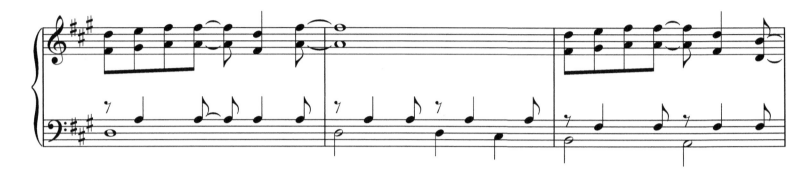

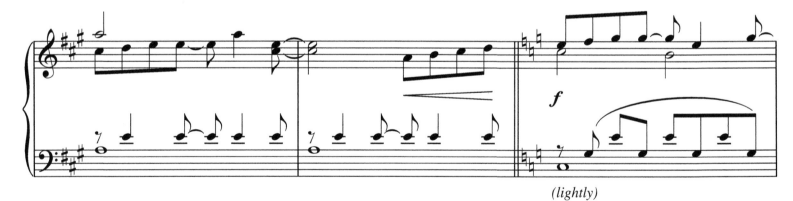

(lightly)

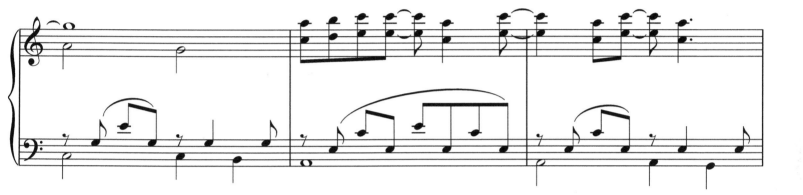

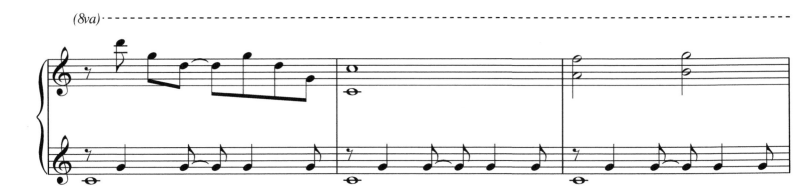

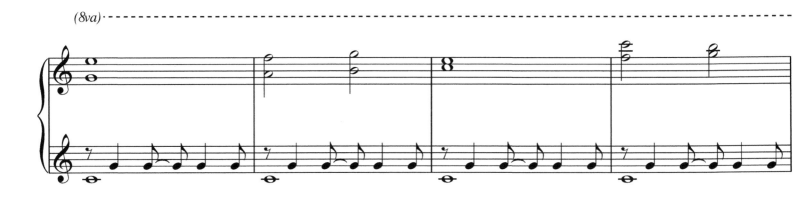

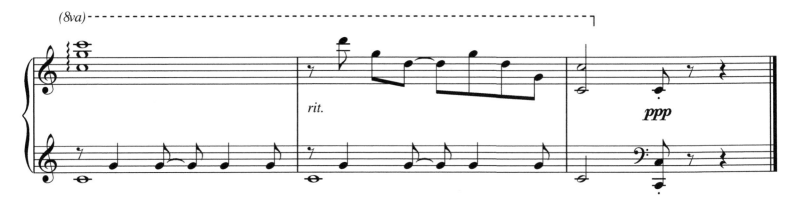

The Heart Asks Pleasure First

from THE PIANO

By Michael Nyman

Allegro, flowing ♩ = 144

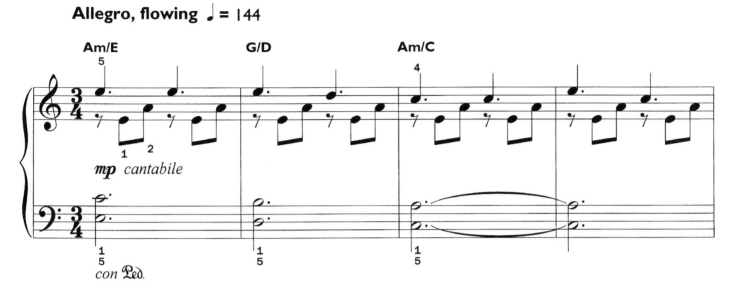

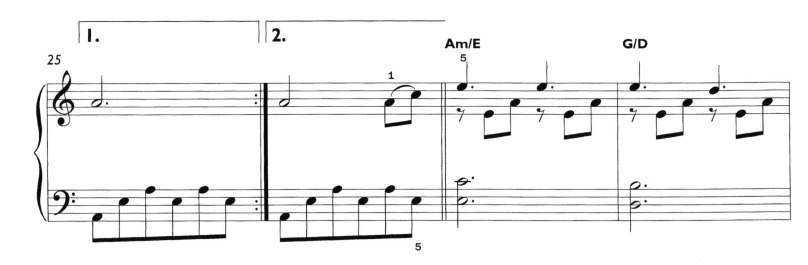

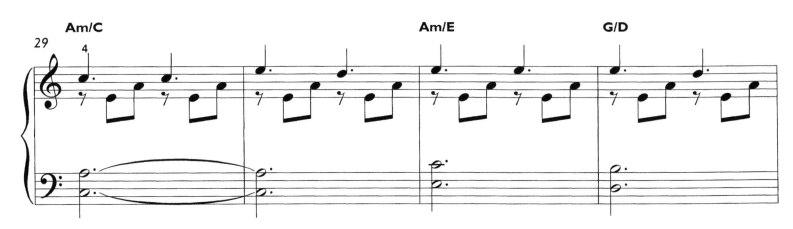

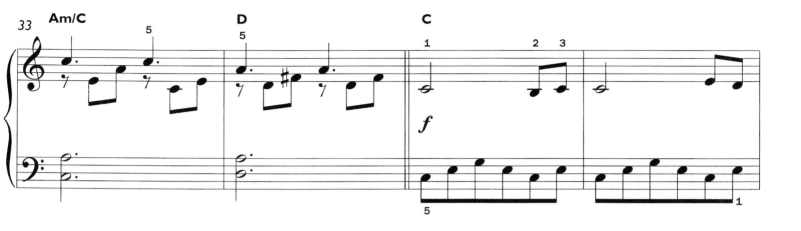

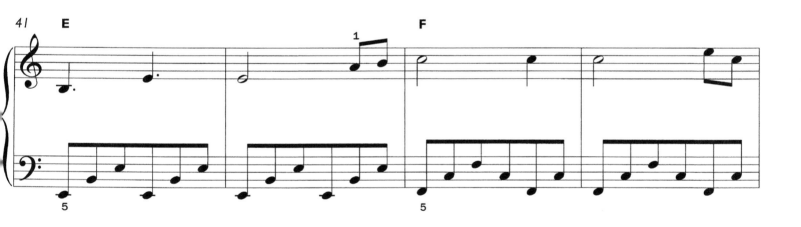

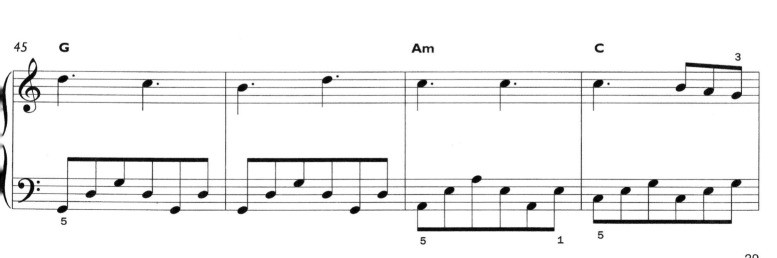

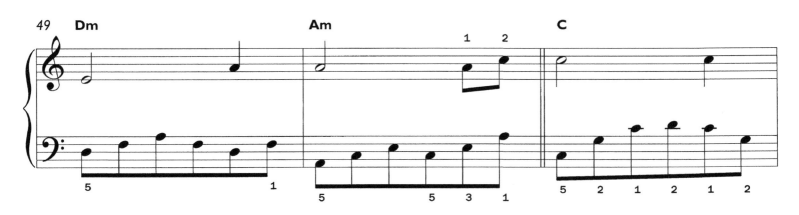

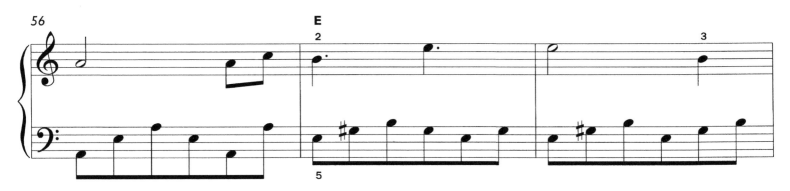

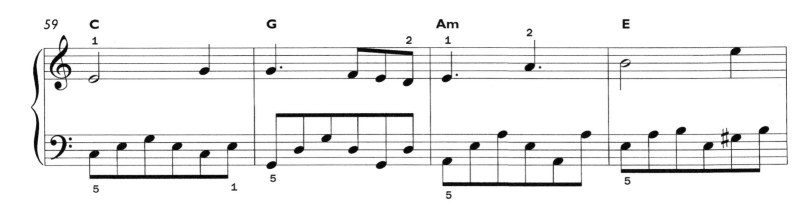

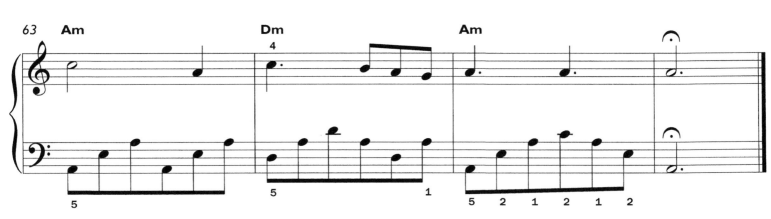

40

Indecent Proposal
(Main Title)
from INDECENT PROPOSAL

By John Barry

Slowly

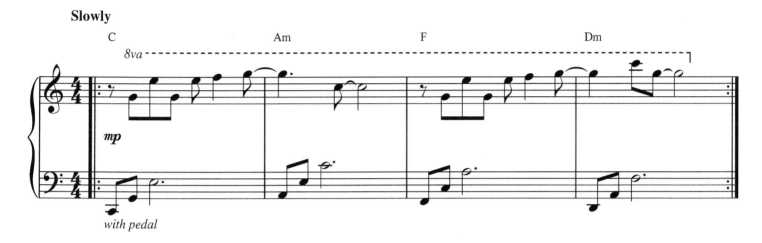

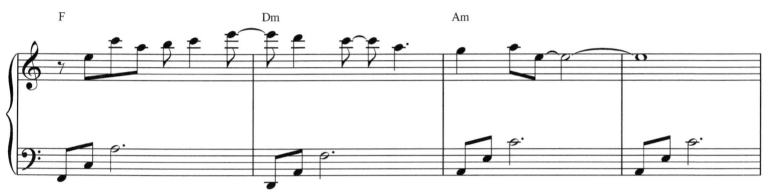

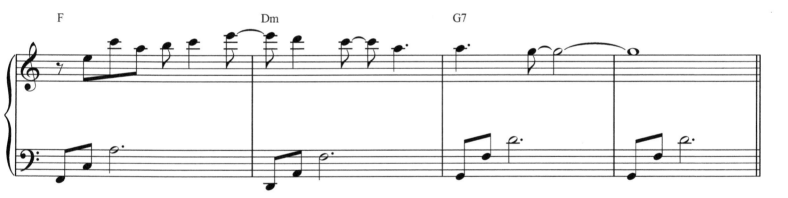

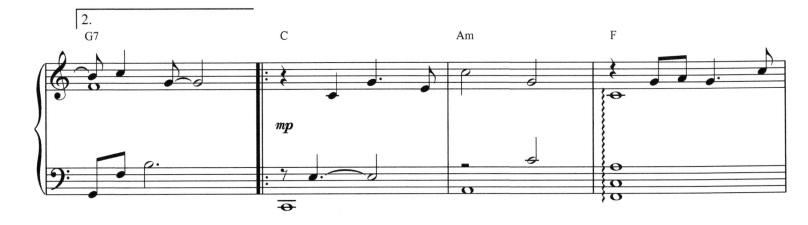

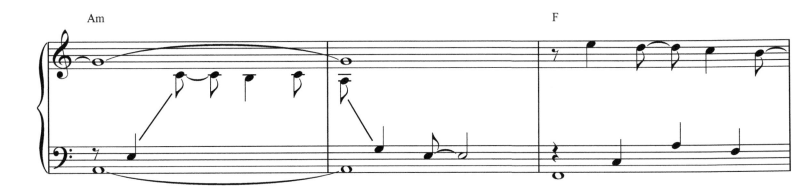

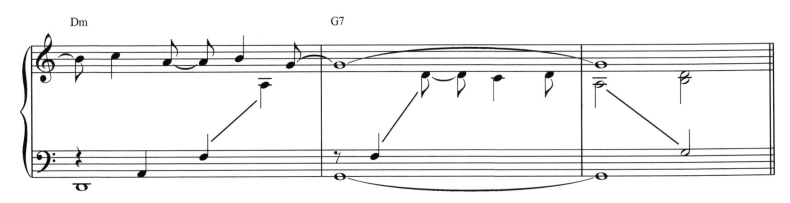

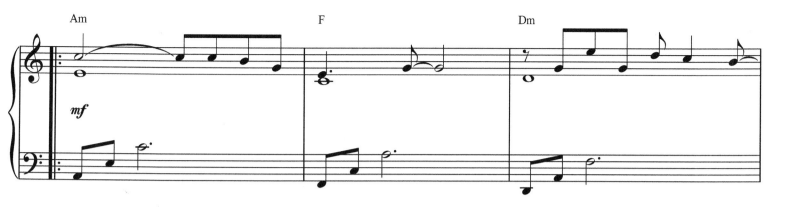

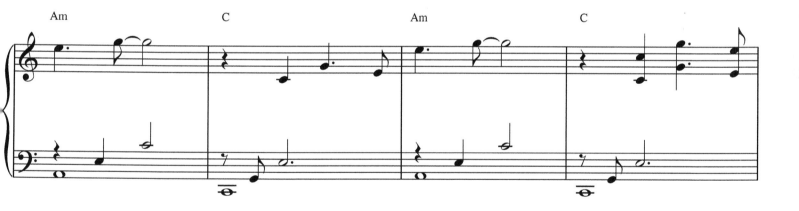

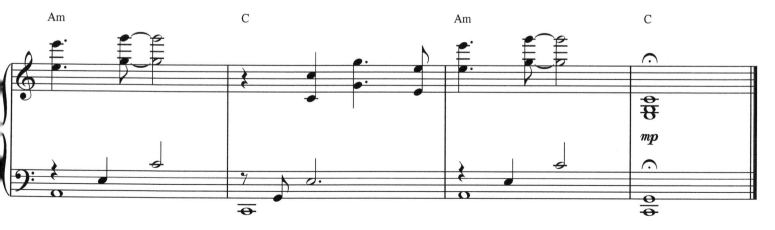

It Might Be You

Theme from TOOTSIE

Words by
Alan and Marilyn Bergman

Music by Dave Grusin

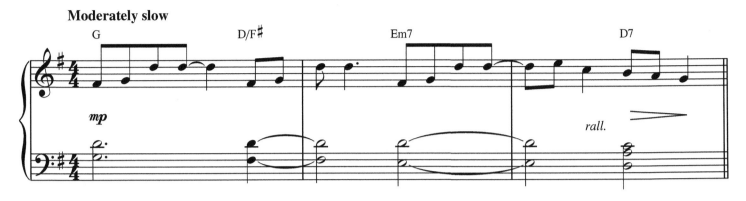

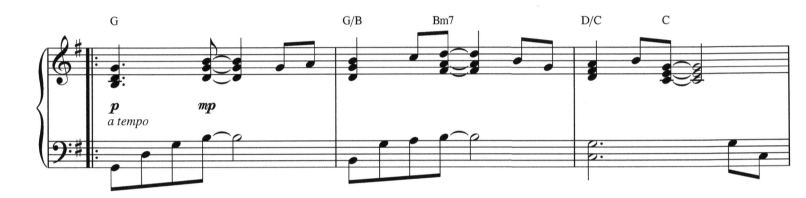

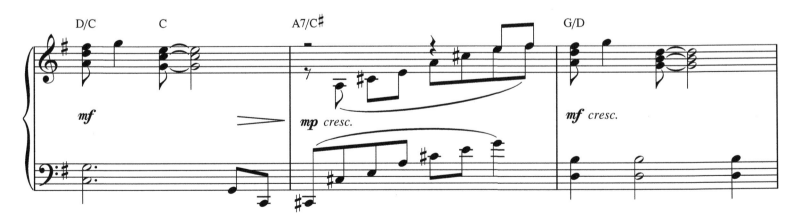

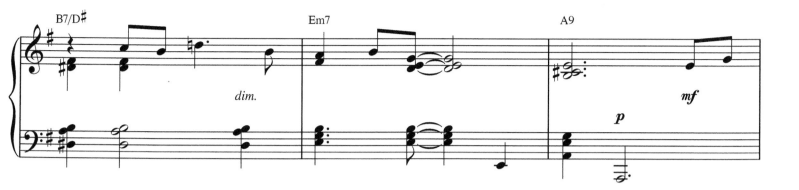

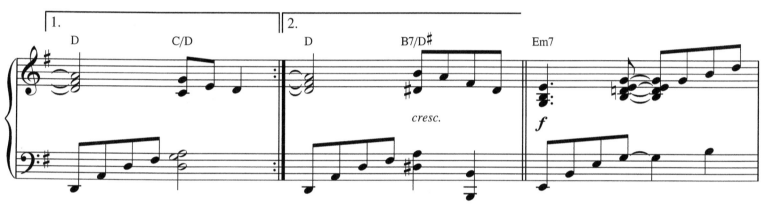

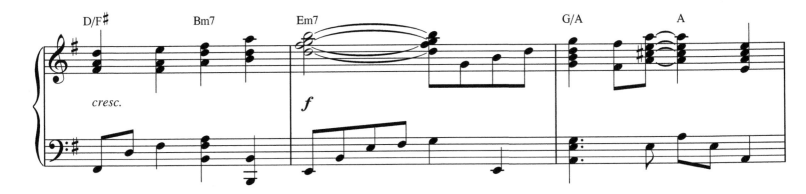

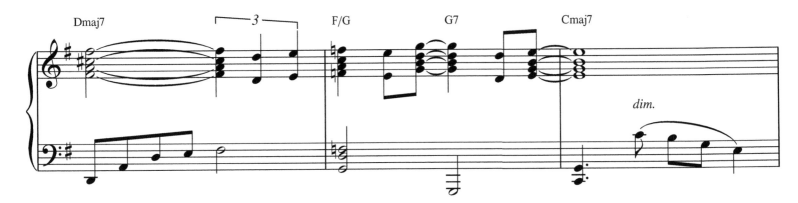

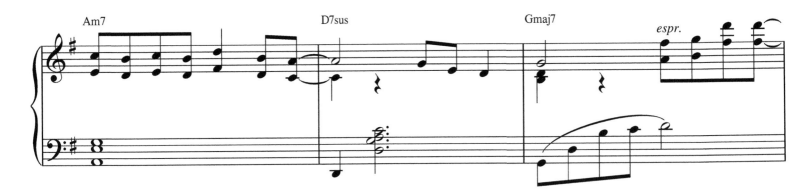

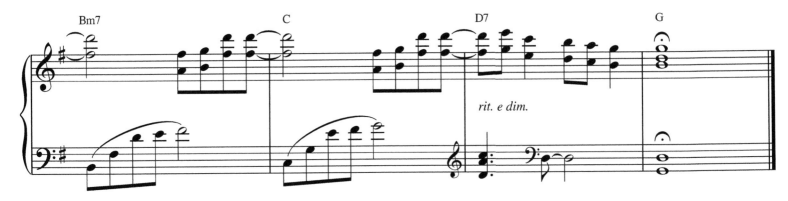

Theme from "Jurassic Park"

from the Universal Motion Picture JURASSIC PARK

Composed by John Williams

48

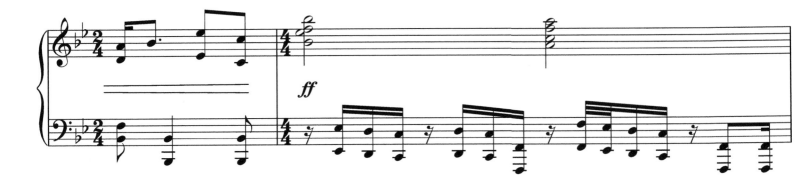

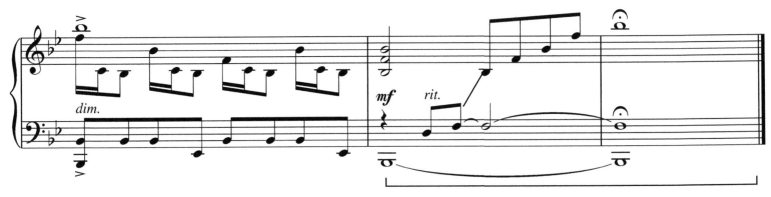

The Ludlows
from TriStar Pictures' LEGENDS OF THE FALL

Composed by James Horner

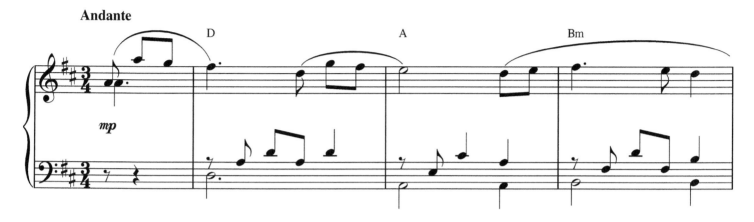

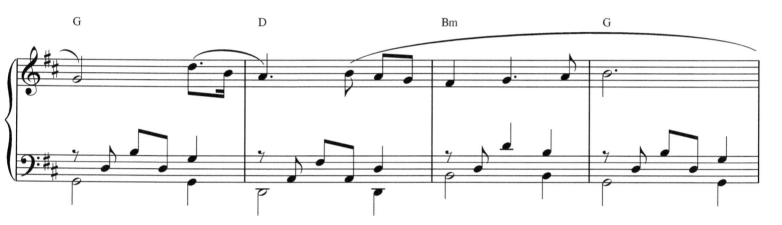

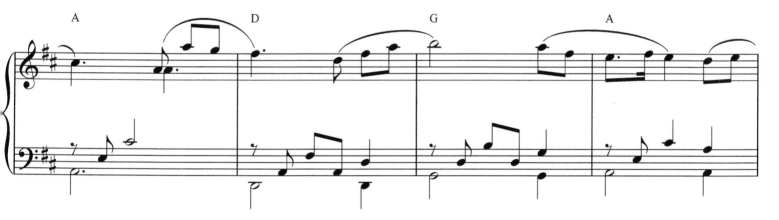

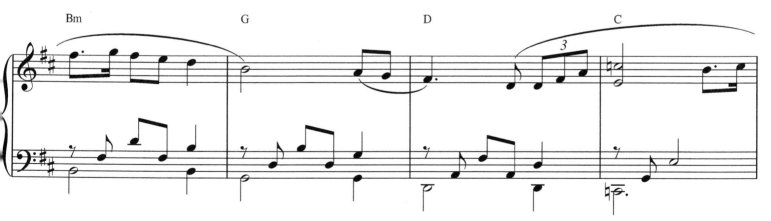

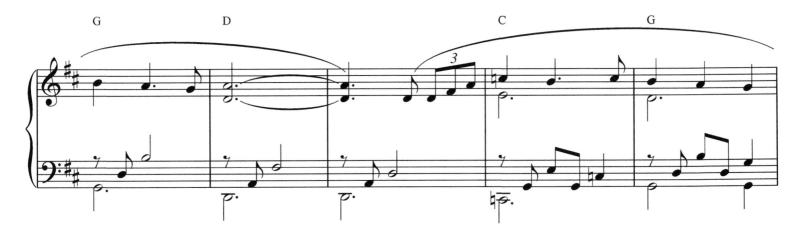

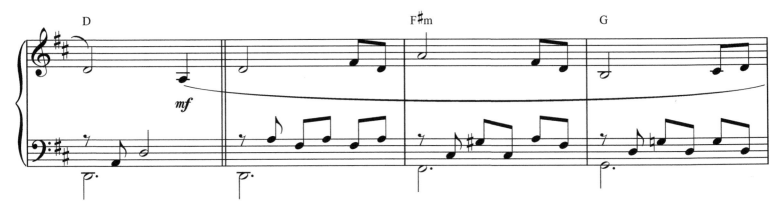

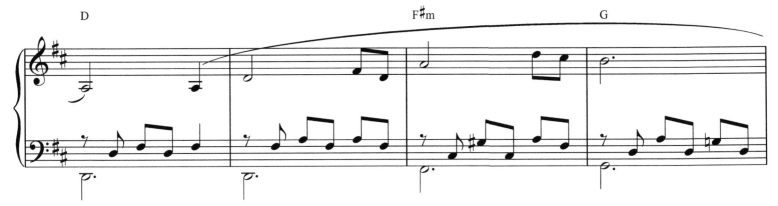

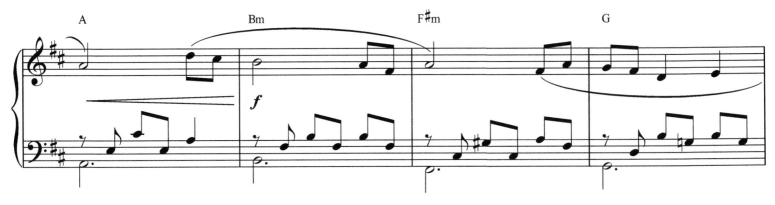

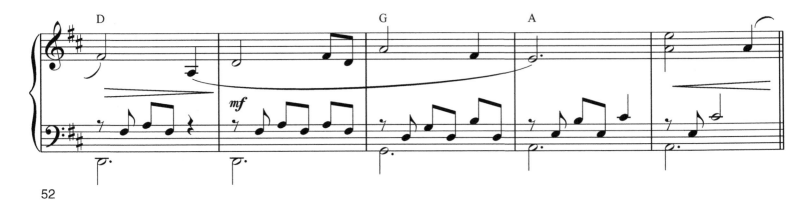

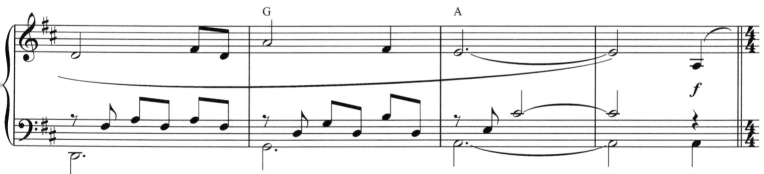

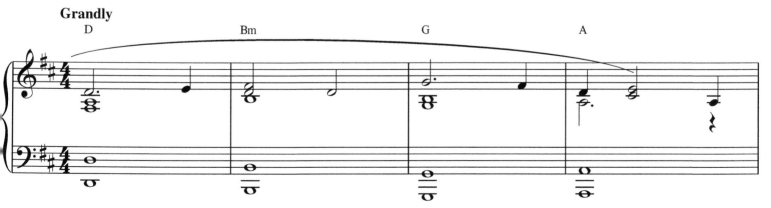

Grandly

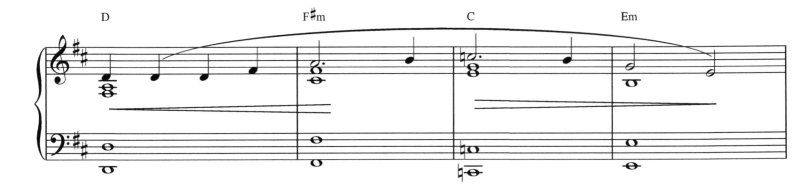

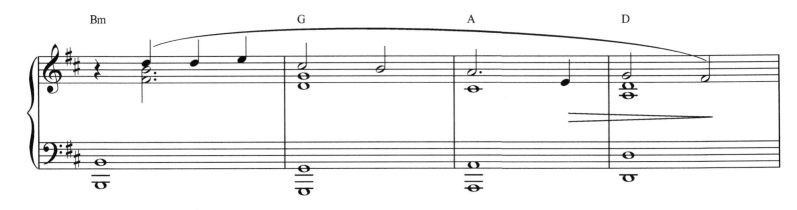

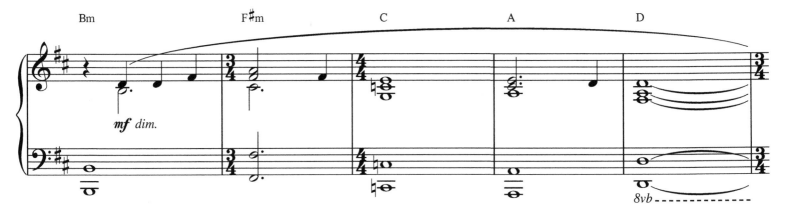

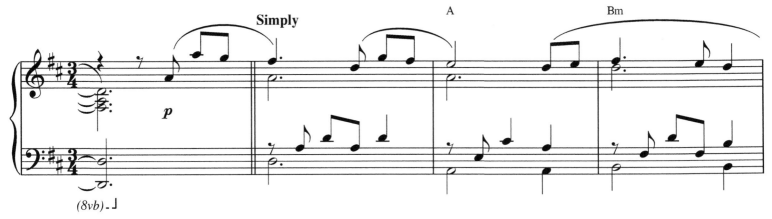

54

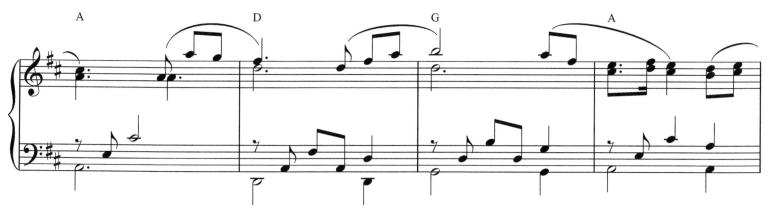

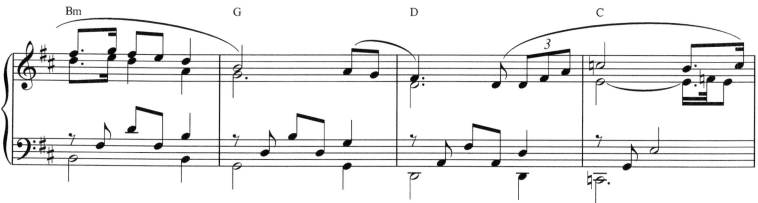

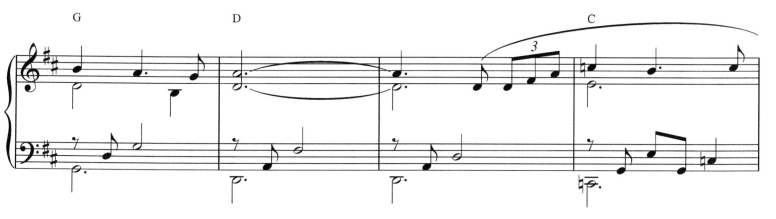

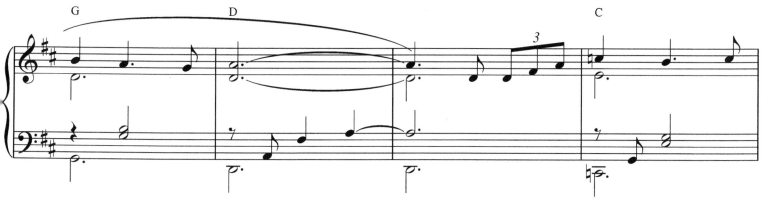

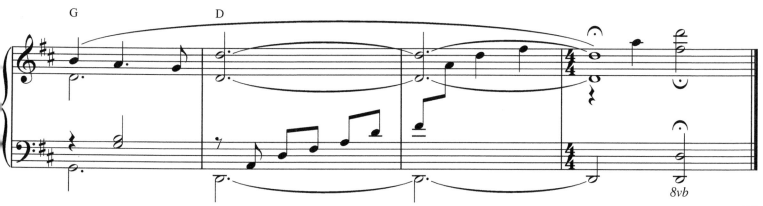

Leaving Netherfield

from PRIDE & PREJUDICE

By Dario Marianelli

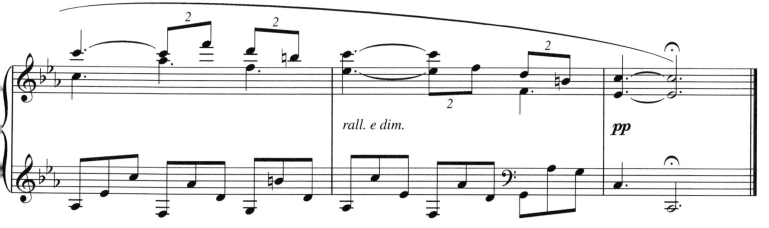

Maestro

from THE HOLIDAY

By Hans Zimmer

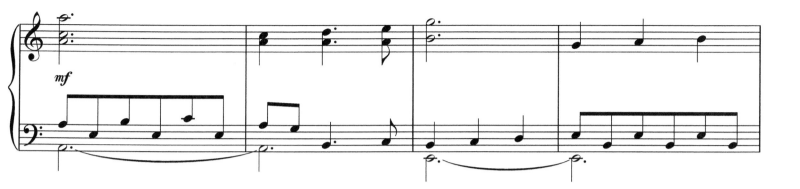

Slowly, in 2

Play 4 times

with pedal

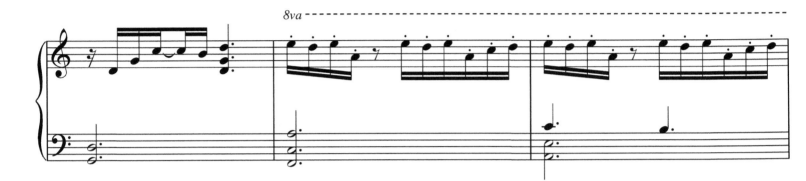

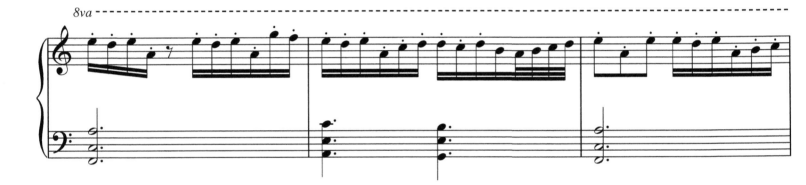

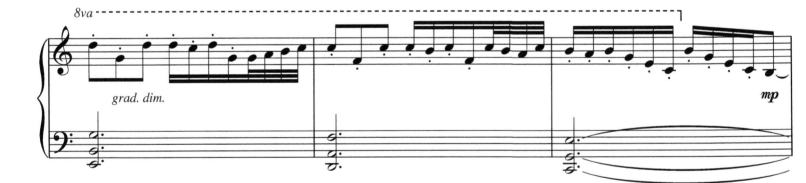

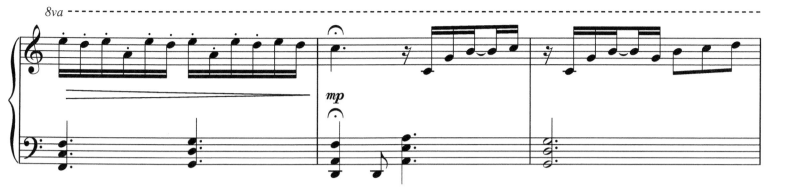

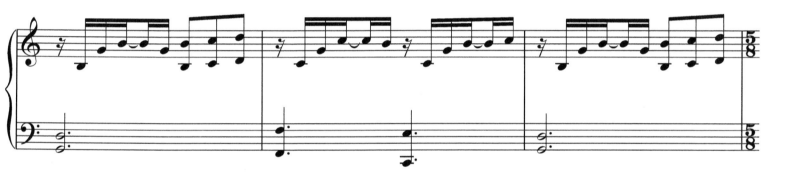

Very slowly

Neverland - Piano Variations in Blue

from FINDING NEVERLAND

By A.P. Kaczmarek

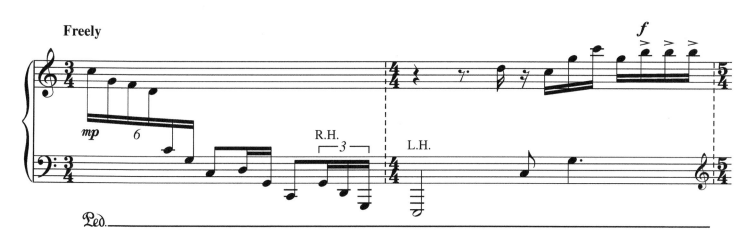

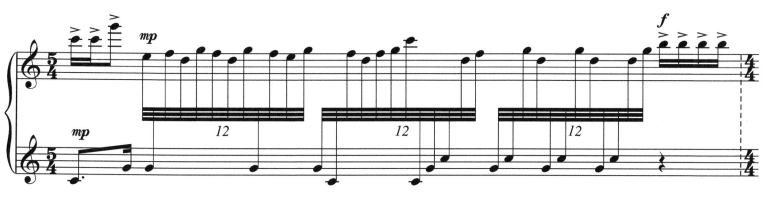

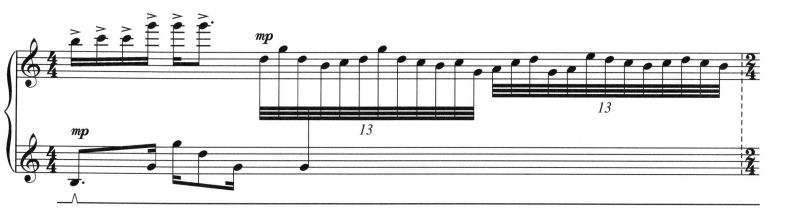

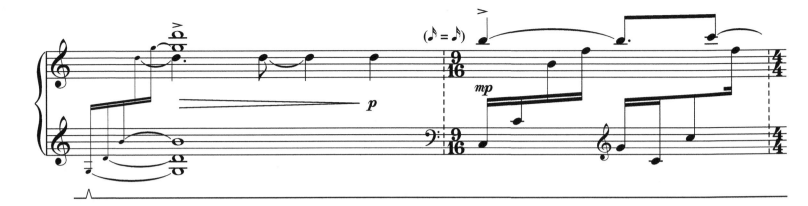

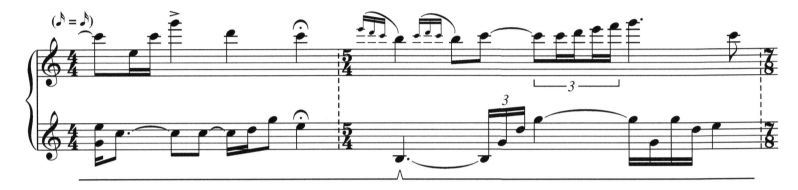

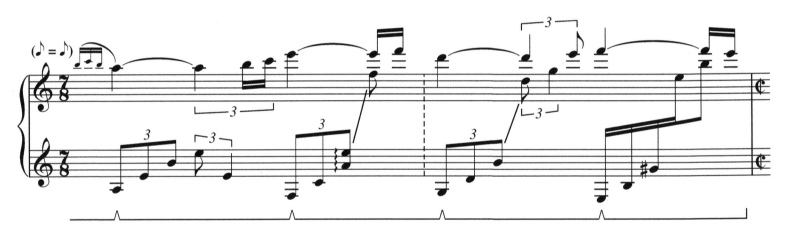

Slowly, freely, in 2

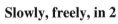

with pedal

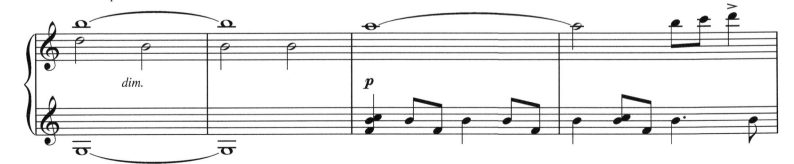

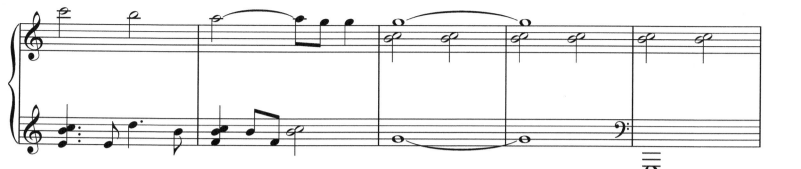

Slowly, in 2 (in time)

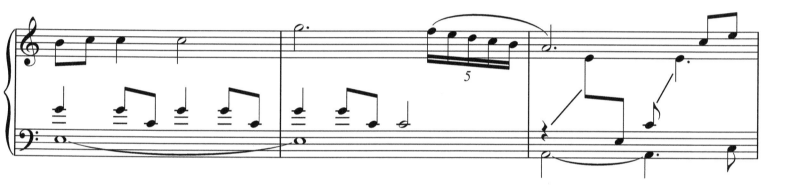

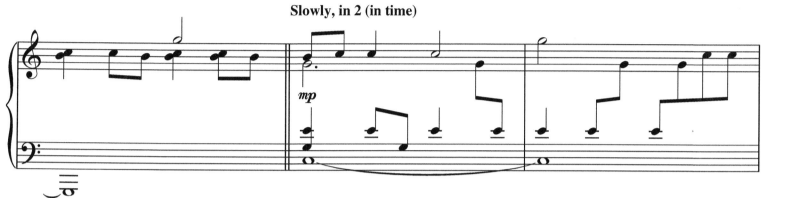

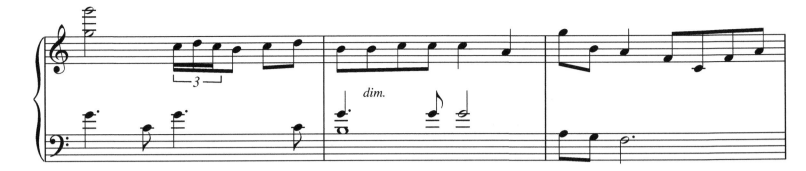

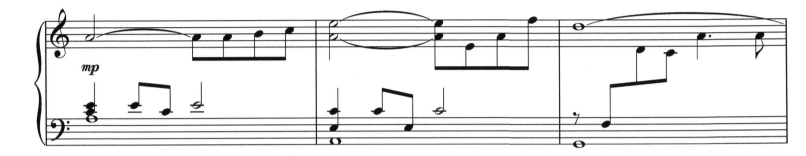

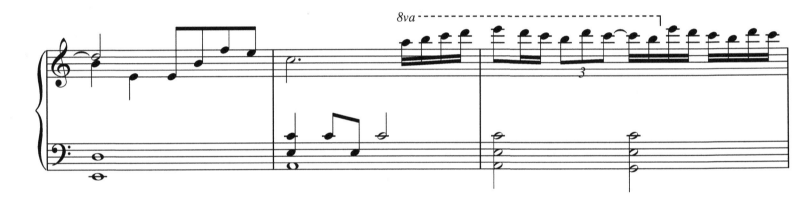

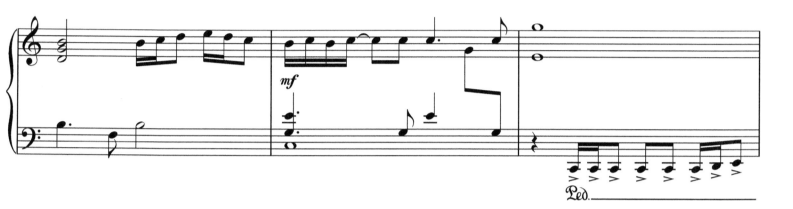

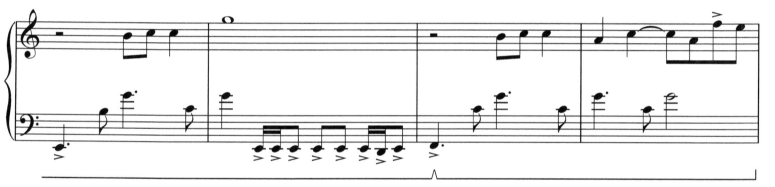

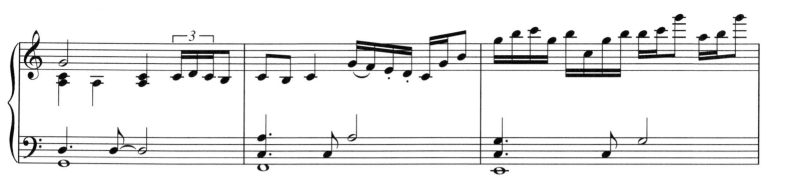

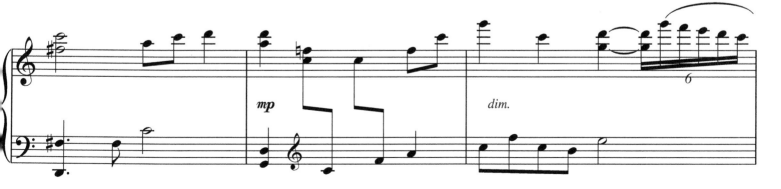

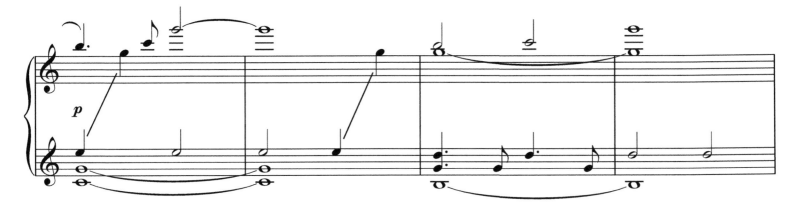

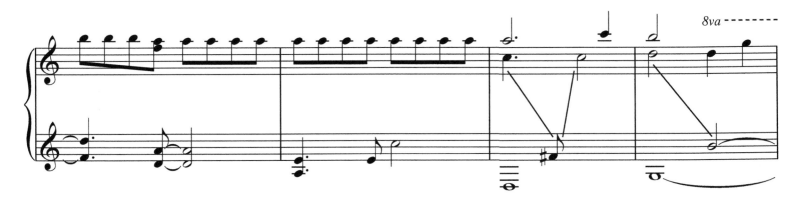

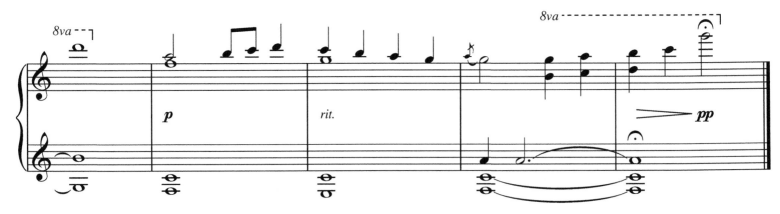

On Golden Pond

Main Theme from ON GOLDEN POND

Music by Dave Grusin

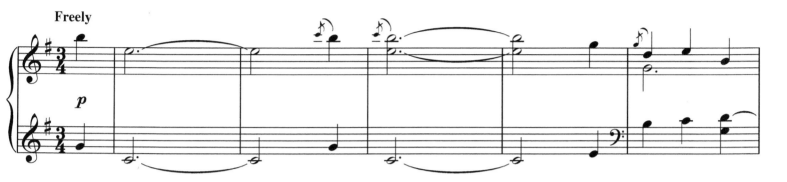

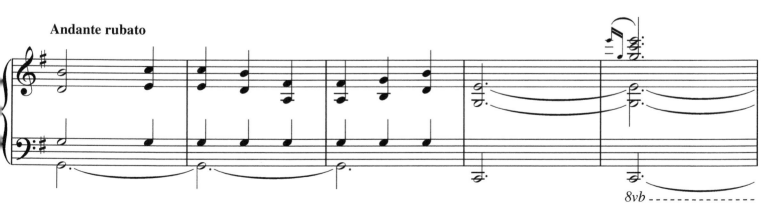

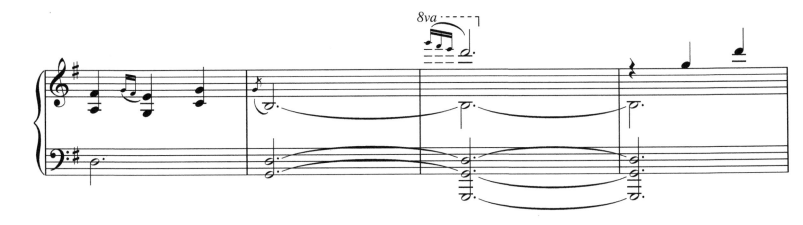

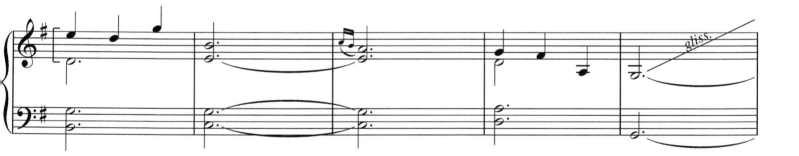

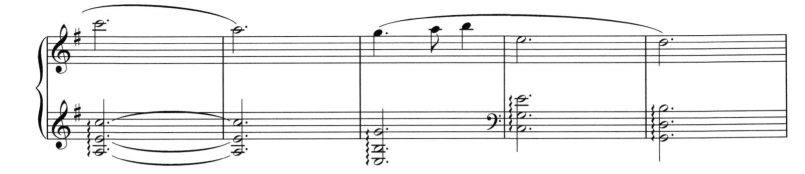

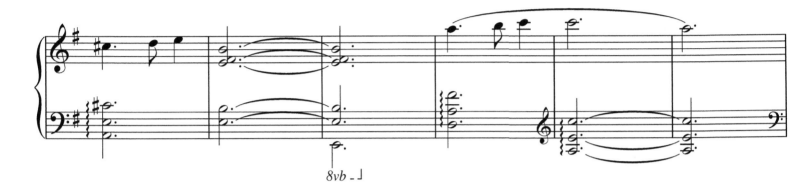

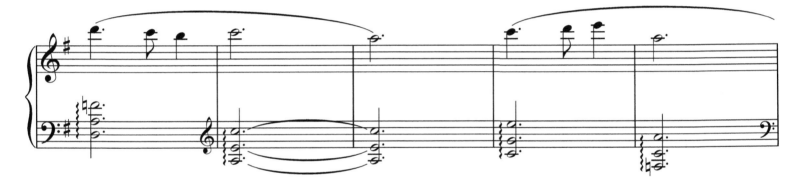

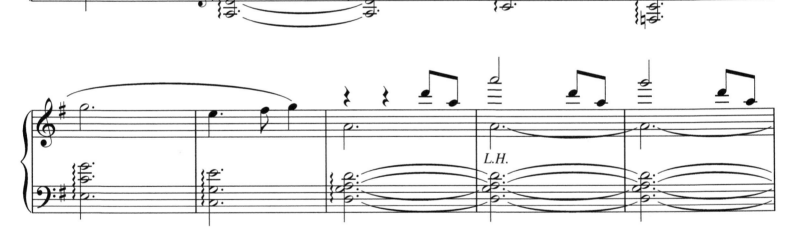

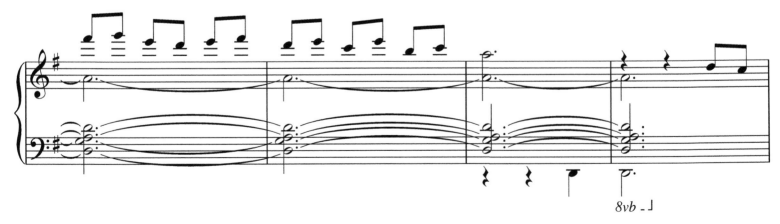

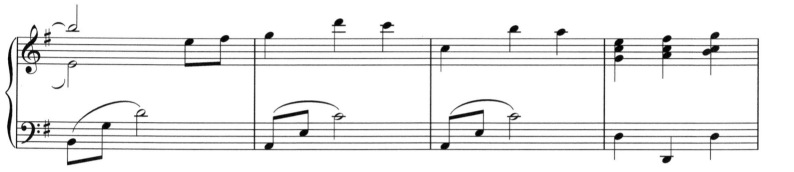

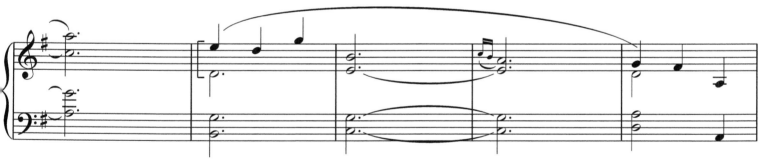

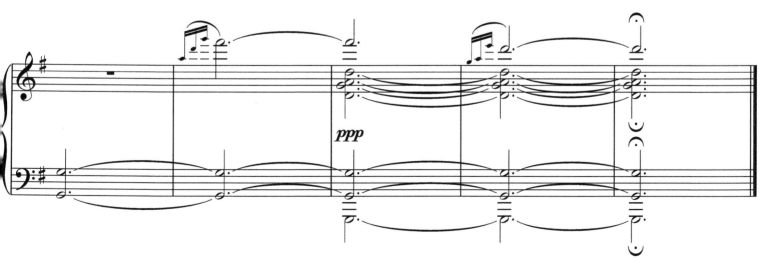

The Piano Duet
from Warner Bros. Pictures' CORPSE BRIDE

Music by Danny Elfman

Secondo

Slowly, freely (♩. = 44)

The Piano Duet

from Warner Bros. Pictures' CORPSE BRIDE

Music by Danny Elfman

Primo

Slowy, freely (♩. = 44)

Secondo

poco rit.   *a tempo*   (Primo cues)

Brightly (♩. = 92)

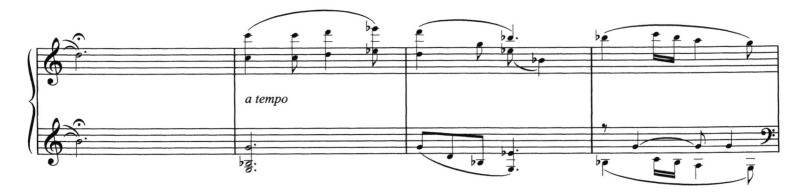

a tempo

78

Primo

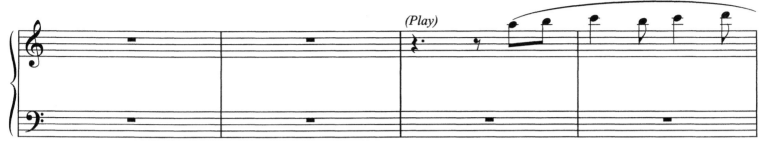

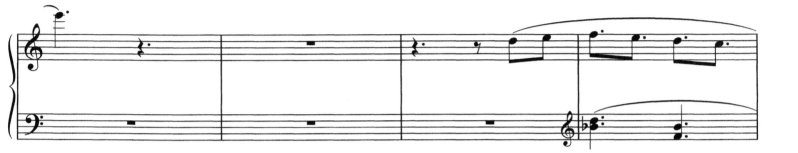

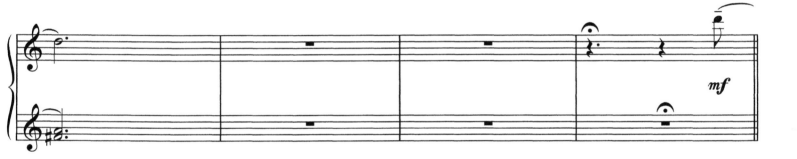

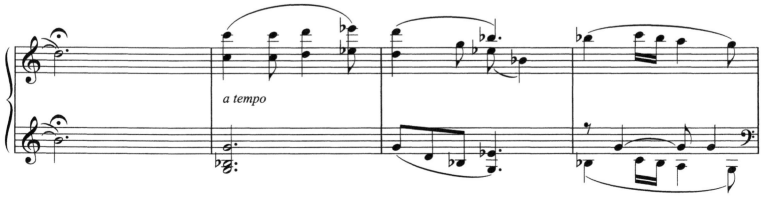

Secondo

Slightly slower (♩. = 80)

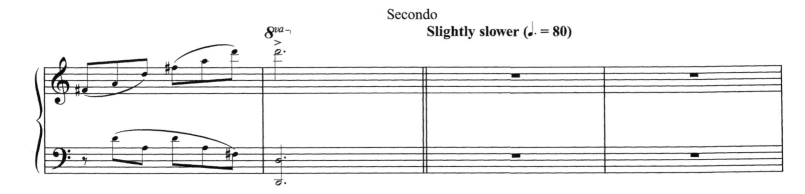

(Play)

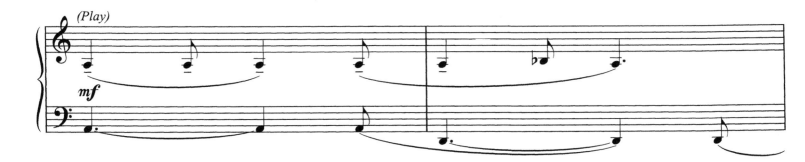

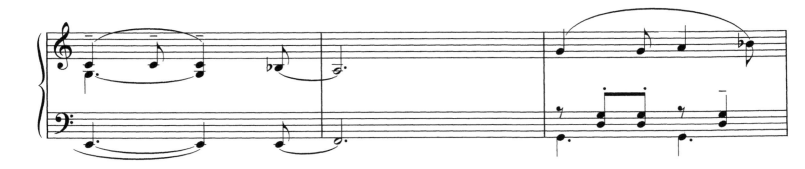

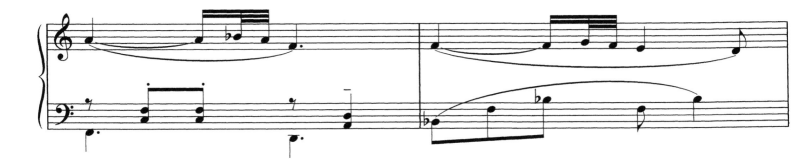

Slightly slower (♩. = 80)

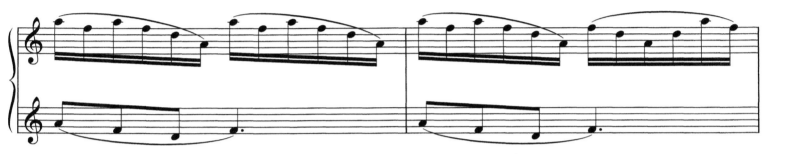

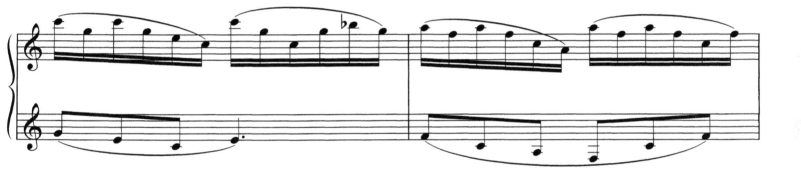

Road to Perdition

from the Motion Picture ROAD TO PERDITION

By Thomas Newman

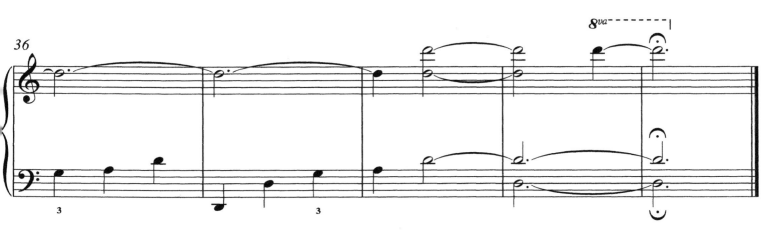

Theme from "Sabrina"

from the Paramount Motion Picture SABRINA

By John Williams

Dreamily

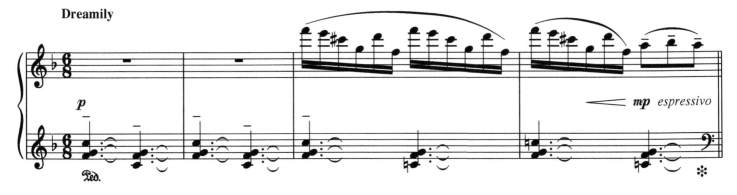

More movement

legato

cresc.

poco rit.

$\boldsymbol{f}$ *espressivo*

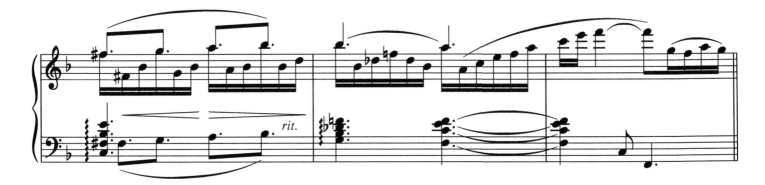

Tempo I

gently

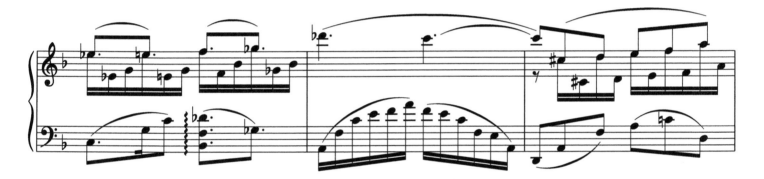

rit.   *a tempo*

rit.

Love Theme from "St. Elmo's Fire"

from the Motion Picture ST. ELMO'S FIRE

Words and Music by
David Foster

Moderately slow

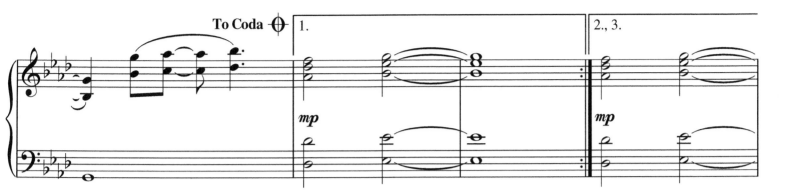

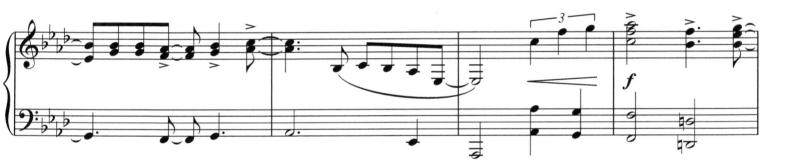

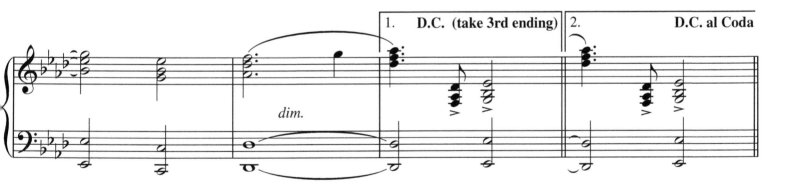

Somewhere in Time

from SOMEWHERE IN TIME

By John Barry

Moderately slow

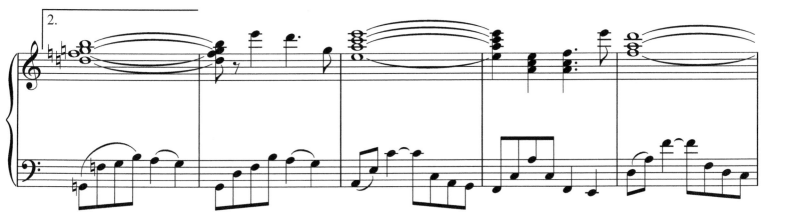

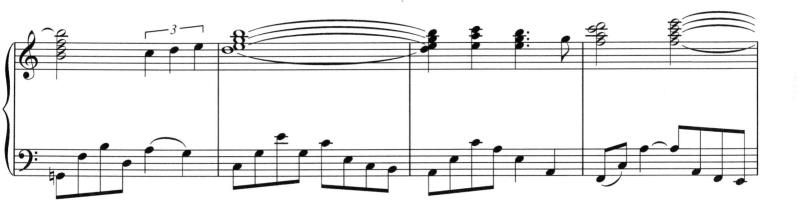

Theme from Summer of '42
(The Summer Knows)

Words and Music by
Michel Legrand

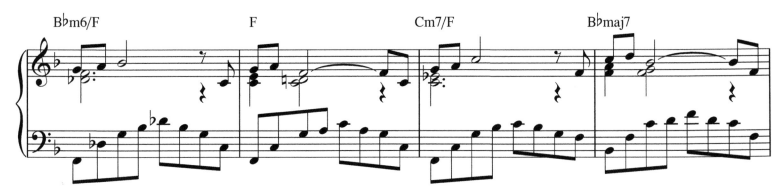

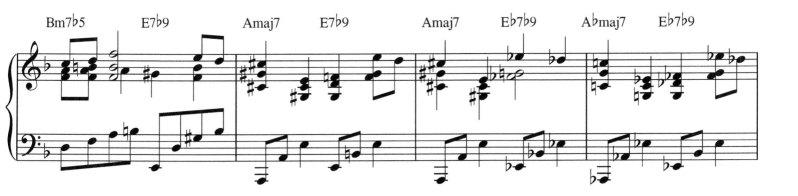

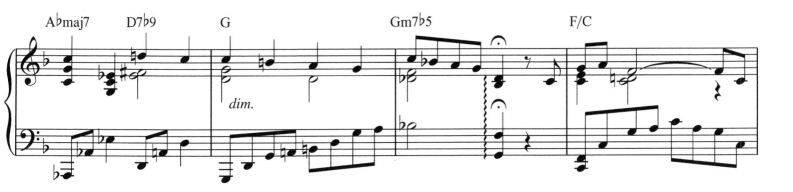

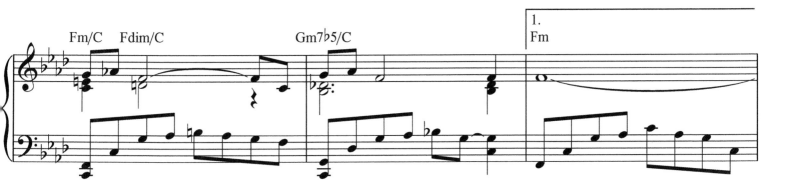

Riverside Walk

from WHILE YOU WERE SLEEPING

Music by Randy Edelman

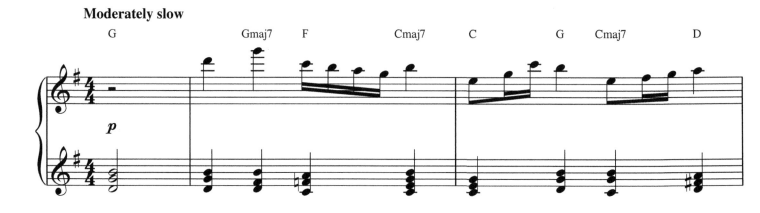

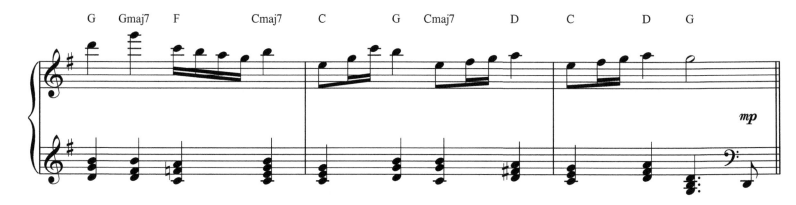

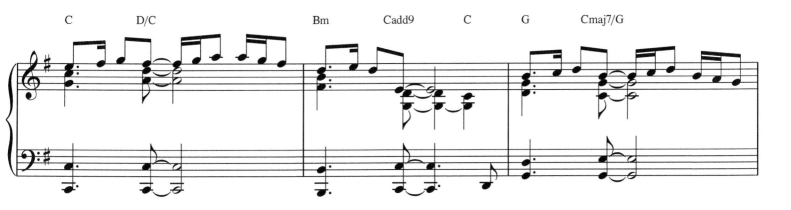

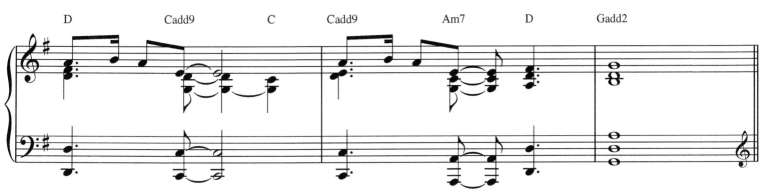

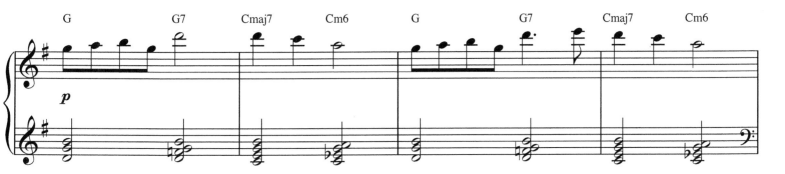

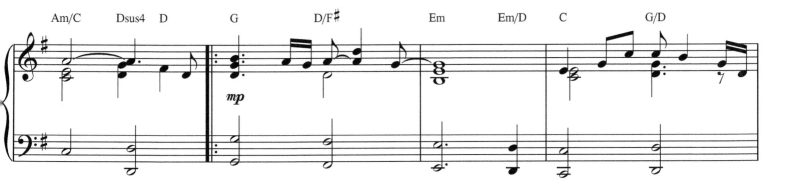

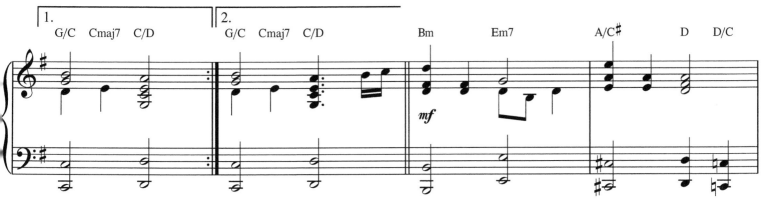

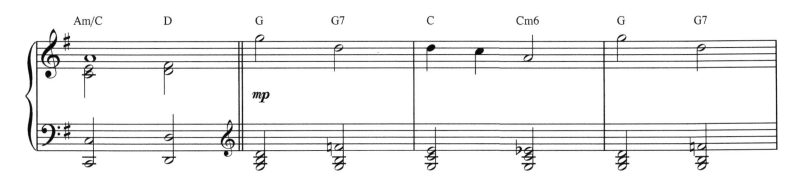

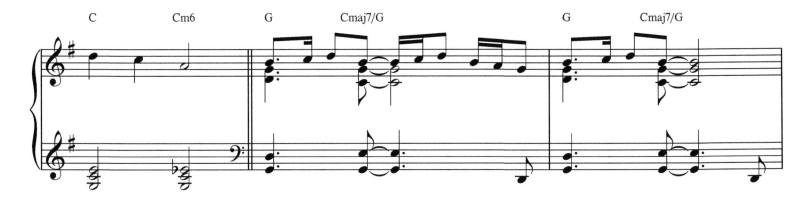

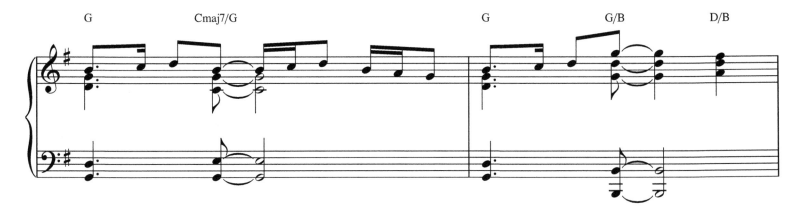

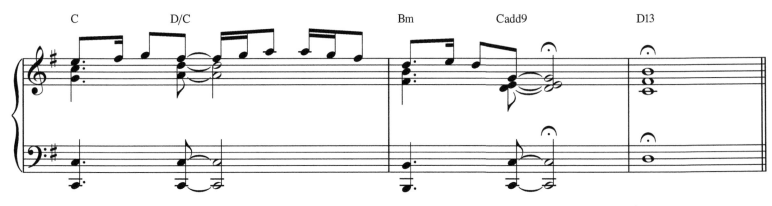

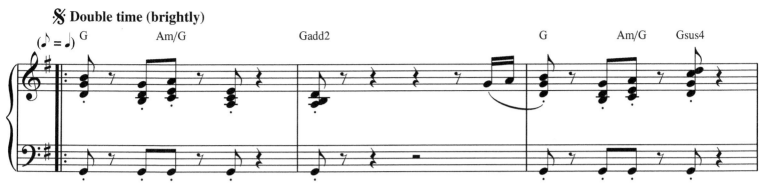

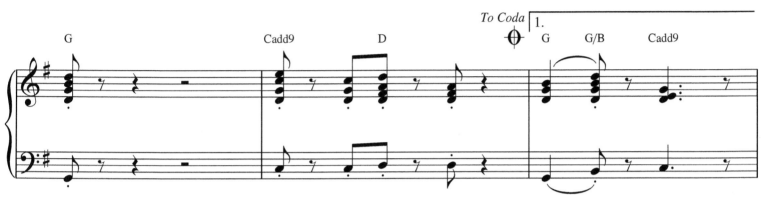

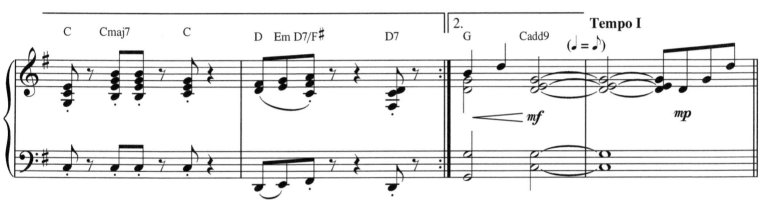

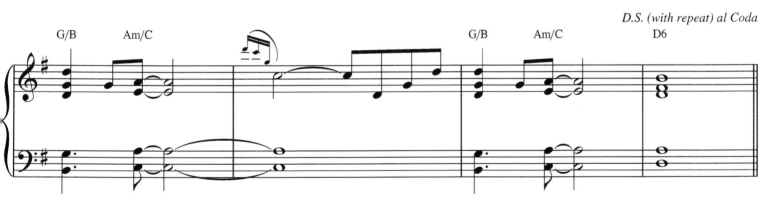

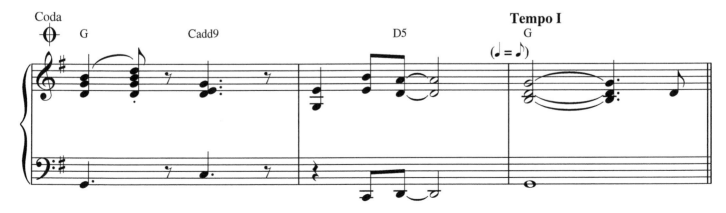

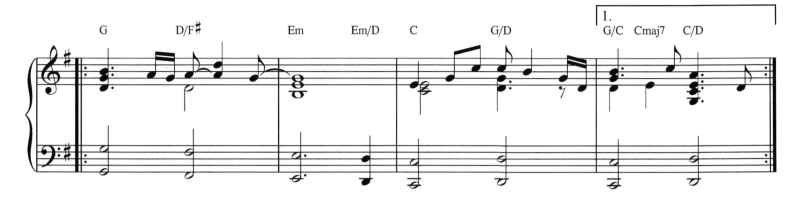

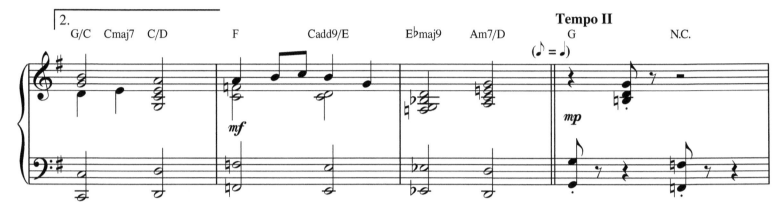

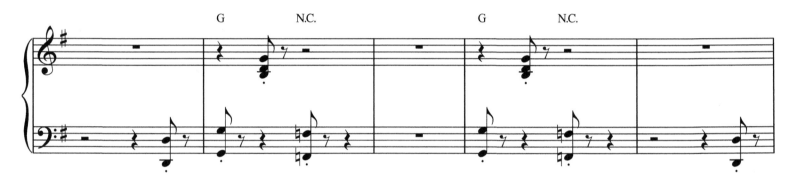

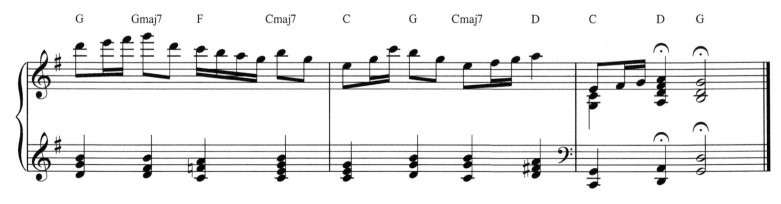

Tubular Bells

Theme from THE EXORCIST

By Mike Oldfield

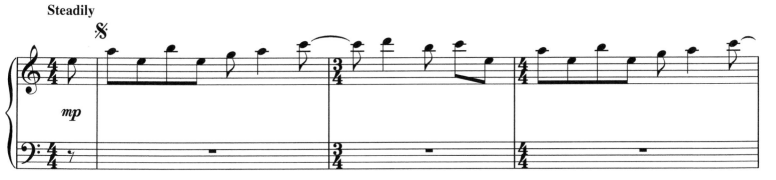

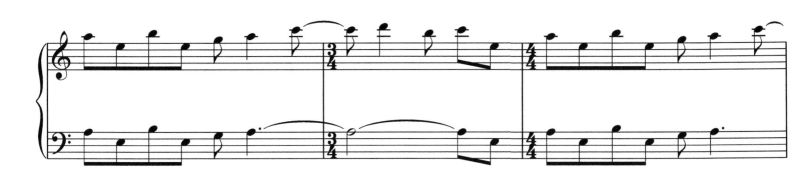

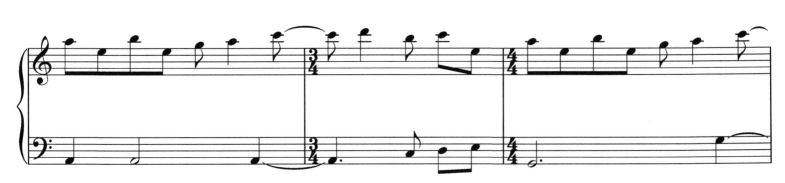

To Coda ⊕

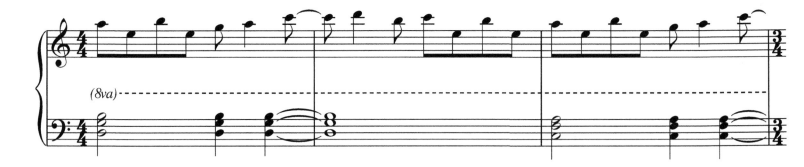

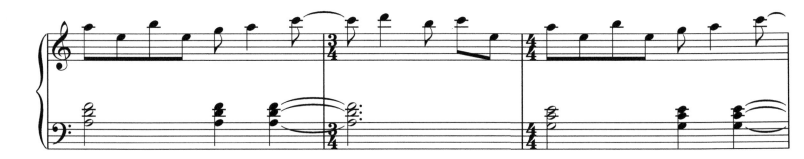

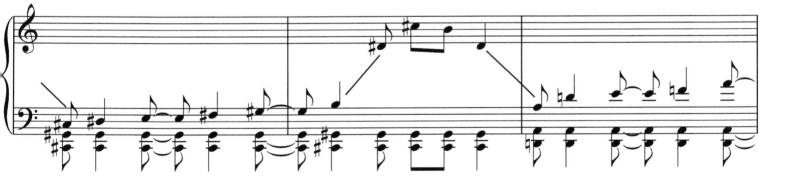

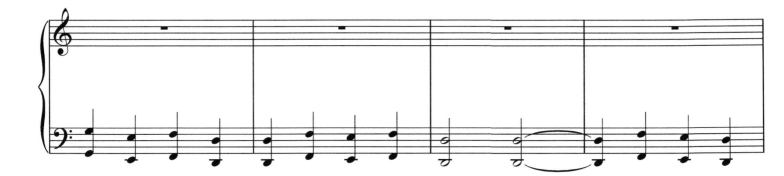

D.S. al Coda

CODA

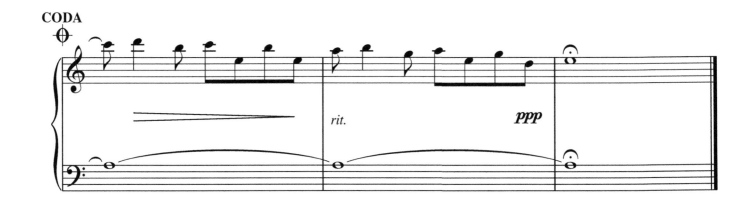